Its sparse shadows are horizontal and
slanted — the water is clear and shallow;
Its hidden fragrance wafts and moves —
the moon is hazy and dim.

LIN BU

To left and right the green
walls were washed
By flying pearls scattering light mist
And streaming foam boiling
round great rocks!

LI BAI

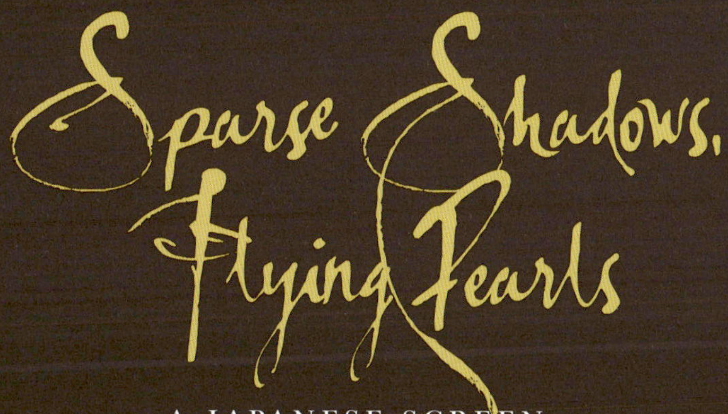

A JAPANESE SCREEN
REVEALED

QUEENSLAND ART GALLERY 2005

Cover:
Unkoku Tōeki Japan 1591–1644
Landscapes with Li Bai and Lin Bu (detail: right-hand screen) c.1610–44 (early Edo period)
Ink, colours and gold wash on paper on six-fold wooden framed screens (*byobu*), edged with woven silk and covered verso in paper relief printed in black
Pair of six-panel screens; 169 x 377.2cm (overall comp.)
Gift of James Fairfax, AO, through the Queensland Art Gallery Foundation 1992
Collection: Queensland Art Gallery

PUBLISHER
Queensland Art Gallery
Melbourne Street, South Brisbane
PO Box 3686, South Brisbane
Queensland 4101 Australia

www.qag.qld.gov.au

National Library of Australia Cataloguing-in-Publication Data:
Tiffin, Sarah.
Sparse shadows, flying pearls : a Japanese screen revealed.

Bibliography.
ISBN 1 876509 02 3.
ISBN 1 876509 91 0 (pbk).

1. Unkoku, Tōeki, 1591-1644 - Criticism and interpretation.
2. Screen painting, Japanese. 3. Screens - Japan.
4. Politics in art. I. Queensland Art Gallery. II. Title.

759.952

SUPPORTED BY

AUSTRALIAN CENTRE OF ASIA-PACIFIC ART

An initiative of the
Queensland Gallery of Modern Art

Published in association with the exhibition 'Sparse Shadows, Flying Pearls: A Japanese Screen Revealed' held at the Queensland Art Gallery 27 August – 27 November 2005.

CURATOR
Sarah Tiffin, Curator, Historical Asian Art

PUBLICATION TEAM
Lynne Seear, Assistant Director (Curatorial and Collection Development)
Ian Were, Senior Editor
Kylie Timmins, Publications Assistant
Elliott Murray, Head of Design
Chris Starr, Senior Designer

Photography: All Queensland Art Gallery Collection works by Ray Fulton. All other photography credited as known.

Printed on Spicers Paper PhoeniXmotion Xenon by Screen Offset Printing, Brisbane, Australia

CONTENTS

JAPANESE AND CHINESE PERIODS AND DYNASTIES 6

MAP OF THE REGION 7

SPARSE SHADOWS, FLYING PEARLS:
A JAPANESE SCREEN REVEALED 8

CATALOGUE OF WORKS 45

SELECTED BIBLIOGRAPHY 46

ACKNOWLEDGMENTS 48

Japanese and Chinese Periods and Dynasties

The terms BCE (Before the Common Era) and CE (the Common Era) are used for BC and AD respectively.

Japan — Periods		
	Jōmon	to c.300BCE
	Yayoi	c.300BCE – c.250CE
	Kofun	c.250–38
	Asuka	538–710
	Nara	710–94
	Heian	794–1185
	Kamakura	1185–1333
	Muromachi	1338–1568
	Momoyama	1568–1615
	Edo	1615–1868
	Meiji	1868–1912
	Taishō	1912–26
	Shōwa	1926–

China — Dynasties/Periods		
	Neolithic	c.3500–1600BCE
	Shang	1600–1046BCE
	Western Zhou	1046–770BCE
	Eastern Zhou	770–256BCE
	Spring and Autumn period	770–476BCE
	Warring States period	475–221BCE
	Qin	221–06BCE
	Han	206BCE – 220CE
	Three Kingdoms	220–65
	Jin	265-420
	Northern and Southern dynasties	420–581
	Sui	581–618
	Tang	618–907
	Five dynasties	907–60
	Song	960–1279
	Liao	916–1125
	Jin	1115–1234
	Yuan	1279–1368
	Ming	1368–1644
	Qing	1644–1911
	Republic	1911–49
	People's Republic	1949–

Sea of
Japan
Edo (modern Tokyo)
JAPAN
Kyoto
Beijing
PACIFIC
OCEAN
East
China
Sea
CHINA
Shanghai
Xihu (West Lake)
Lushan

Sparse Shadows, Flying Pearls: A Japanese Screen Revealed

Unkoku Tōeki
Japan 1591–1644
Landscapes with Li Bai and Lin Bu (detail: right-hand screen) c.1610–44 (early Edo period)
Ink, colours and gold wash on paper on six-fold wooden framed screens (*byobu*), edged with woven silk and covered verso in paper relief printed in black
Pair of six-panel screens; 169 x 377.2cm (overall comp.)
Gift of James Fairfax, AO, through the Queensland Art Gallery Foundation 1992
Collection: Queensland Art Gallery

Why do I live among the green mountains?
I laugh and answer not. My soul is serene.
It dwells in another heaven and earth belonging to no man —
The peach trees are in flower, and the water flows on . . .
Li Bai[1]

The very handsome pair of six-fold screens in the Queensland Art Gallery Collection painted by the Japanese artist Unkoku Tōeki (1591–1644) depicts two Chinese poets — Li Bai (701–62)[2] and Lin Bu (967–1028),[3] with their attendants, amidst an imagined, idealised Chinese landscape.

The influence of Chinese cultural models is apparent in the identity of the figures, their remote and mountainous settings, and the manner of their depiction. This is heavily influenced by both Chinese ink painting and the work of the celebrated fifteenth-century Japanese painter Sesshū (1420–1506), whose work informed the Unkoku house style.[4] Sesshū had been a seminal figure in the development of Chinese-influenced ink painting (*suiboku-ga*) in Japan, and the Unkoku School claimed a close affiliation with him thanks to its founder, Tōeki's father Tōgan (1547–1618), who was much admired for his ability to emulate Sesshū's Sinicised painting style.[5]

Having served as Tōgan's apprentice for some years and collaborating with him on a number of projects before succeeding him as head of the School in 1618, Tōeki's own style bears his father's influence. In the Gallery's screens, strong, bold outlines define the three main elements: Li Bai standing at the cliff edge in the right foreground, gazing, as he does in so many Chinese and Japanese depictions, in rapt admiration at an elegant waterfall; Lin Bu seated in his simple, unpretentious pavilion beneath a craggy overhang in the left foreground; and at the centre of the screens, the falls which attract Li Bai's attention.

The monumental scale of the screens readily accommodates the generous expanse of space that unites the separate sections of the composition. Pale, delicate washes depicting gently diffused mountain ranges and valleys of ethereal, mist-shrouded pines indicate the vagueness of distance and create a sense of recession. The framing elements of the trees, rock escarpments and scattered boulders in the right and left foregrounds are given solidity, texture and definition by the tonal gradations of grey infill and the short, deft, horizontal brushstrokes and softer dabs of ink which animate their surfaces. Small touches of colour — lacquer reds, sombre grey-greens, and chalky whites — are repeated across both screens to produce a harmonising effect.

While adopting a number of the techniques of the ink-painting tradition employed by his father, Tōeki invigorated the Unkoku School style by introducing a greater emphasis on decorative effect.[6] This mannered approach is evident in the Gallery's screens in his treatment of the falls, particularly in the simple, sweeping curves which define the slopes on either side, and the delicate arabesques of swirling mist which rise between them. The stylised arcs of each hill, which contrast with the jagged contours of the solid, angular rocks in the screen's foreground, are echoed in the repeated undercut of the cliffs. Slicing horizontally across the motif and partially obscuring the falls, the sinuous reach of the pine is anchored by the small tree growing to its left and further balanced by the addition of a line that extends the hill on the left towards the upper-left corner of the screen. A small stand of pines at the brow of the slope distorts and magnifies the scale of the falls.

In his choice of subject matter for the screens and their mode of depiction, Tōeki was referencing the theme of scholarly reclusion, a subject that had its origins in China but which had long figured in Japanese painting, becoming particularly popular during the Momoyama (1568–1615) and early Edo (1615–1868) periods. The iconography of the Gallery's screens, when interpreted against the backdrop of the political intrigues and struggles of the period, can provide a fascinating insight into the way these objects would have been perceived and understood.

Screens were introduced to Japan from China, where they had been in use since at least the Warring States period (475–221BCE). From their earliest arrival in Japan (the first recorded mention in Japanese sources is in the eighth century, regarding a gift to the court from Korea presented in 686), screens were avidly adopted as an important format for painting. Indeed, they were embraced with such skill and enthusiasm that the painted folding screen became an art form that is today more thoroughly associated with Japan than with China.[7]

Folding screens were very costly and desirable objects, found only in the most wealthy homes and institutions. As well as being pleasing to the eye, folding screens served a number of practical functions within the often vast open-plan audience halls that were characteristic of Japanese architecture in the Momoyama and Edo periods. They could be used to block drafts — the Japanese term for folding screens, *byobu*, literally means 'barrier' or 'protection' (*byo*) from 'wind' (*bu*) — or to partition off small areas within the hall to afford privacy. Light, portable and easily stored, screens were readily interchangeable; they could be selected and installed according to the season or occasion, or to create an appropriate ambience or tone, and often served as a backdrop for a figure of authority or rank as they sat before an assembled audience.

Given that reception halls were very important spaces for the enunciation of power, status and aspiration, the screen performed a psychological as much as a physical role, creating a space that was at once both real and idealised.[8] When framed by a screen, its patron–owner was provided with an alternate reality. For the assembled audience, the owner and screen became as one, the three-dimensionality of the screens allowing the boundaries between reality and representation to blur and fade.[9] The owner became metaphorically absorbed into the screen's imagery, intimately associating them with its message and ideals to which an assembled audience would have been acutely attuned.

In discussing the many instances in which Japanese screens like the Gallery's depict Chinese scholars or worthies, modern writers have often emphasised the didactic potential of the imagery. This could provide those in authority in Japan with exemplars of the moral virtue and correct conduct they should emulate in the governance of their domains.

There is, however, another reading of the association between owner and screen, one which emphasises a rapport or correlation between the two. According to this interpretation, the purpose of the screens was not so much to instruct the individual on the appropriate behaviour of a ruler, but to present a visual expression of the patron–owner's own scholarly refinement, sophistication and erudition to an assembled audience.[10]

The idea that the Gallery's screens might have created an idealised, politicised space is particularly significant when we consider the importance placed on the attributes of the poet–recluse within the complex, dynamic and highly competitive political milieu of late sixteenth- and early seventeenth-century Japan. From this perspective, it is apparent that the screens were not merely beautifully rendered depictions of a romanticised China that gave great pleasure to those who viewed them. They also had the potential to communicate messages of great significance to their owner and audience, messages which varied according to circumstance and which could be as relevant to those who held power as those who were denied it. In doing so, the screens underscore how thoroughly the idea of reclusion — its subtleties, complexities, contradictions and ambiguities — was embedded in the culture of Momoyama and early Edo Japan.

Ever parted from the world of men

Unkoku Tōeki
Landscapes with Li Bai and Lin Bu (detail: right-hand screen) c.1610–44 (early Edo period)

The Tang dynasty poet Li Bai (the subject of the right-hand screen) is one of the great figures of Chinese literary history whose prestige as a poet, even during his own lifetime, was considerable. His achievement in becoming a pre-eminent figure of Tang poetry is truly significant considering he was dominant during a 'golden age' of Chinese poetry that was as prolific as it was brilliant.[11]

Tōeki's depiction of Li Bai's obvious appreciation of the waterfall is a reference to one of his best known and best loved poems, *Waterfall at Lu Shan*:

When, west, I climbed Incense Brazier Peak,
I southward saw curtained cataracts

Then roar through dales several miles away;
Sudden as if flying lightning came
But mystic, too, as white rainbows rose:
At first I feared Milky Way had dropped
And sprinkled stars, falling through the clouds!

As I looked up they increased in force,
So mighty was the Creator's work:
An ocean wind blew there without cease,
The river moon gave skies back their light,
The skies in which random torrents rushed;
To left and right the green walls were washed
By flying pearls scattering light mist
And streaming foam boiling round great rocks!

Let me travel to those Glorious Peaks
Where I may feel peace grow in my heart:
I'll have no need more for magic draughts
For I may there wash dust from my face
And enjoy there lodging that I love,
Ever parted from the world of men![12]

Unkoku Tōeki
Landscapes with Li Bai and Lin Bu (detail: left-hand screen) c.1610–44 (early Edo period)

Lin Bu was a poet of the Northern Song dynasty who lived in quiet reclusion on Xihu (West Lake) in south-east China. He achieved a degree of fame for his poetry in praise of the *mei* or flowering plum (*Prunus momei*), especially a couplet drawn from his verse *Small flowering plum in the garden on the hill*:

> Its sparse shadows are horizontal and slanted —
> the water is clear and shallow;
> Its hidden fragrance wafts and moves —
> the moon is hazy and dim.[13]

These lines were singled out for effusive praise by Song critics, firmly establishing Lin Bu's couplet in the literary and painterly tradition of the flowering plum.[14] 'Sparse shadows' and 'hidden fragrance' became familiar metaphors for the plum blossom,[15] and the couplet was frequently quoted, alluded to and depicted by generations of poets, calligraphers and painters.[16]

At first glance it would seem that Li Bai and Lin Bu had little in common. They lived under different dynasties more than two centuries apart and were men of very dissimilar temperament — indeed, it would probably be hard to find two more different personalities than the flamboyant Li Bai and the reticent Lin Bu. Moreover, while Li Bai was a major figure in Chinese cultural history, Lin Bu's talent was more modest. Despite his couplet becoming one of the most frequently quoted homages to the plum, Lin Bu is considered a relatively obscure figure amongst China's literary luminaries.[17]

The two men do, however, share one aspect of their lives that distinguishes them from the vast majority of China's literati. Since the time of the Han dynasty (206BCE – 220CE), nearly every poet with any claim to merit had either served, or aspired to serve, as political functionaries within China's civil service. Lin Bu and Li Bai were notable exceptions.

The fundamental importance that Chinese society placed on participation in the civil service cannot be overstated. During both the Tang and the Song dynasties, China was heavily bureaucratised and participation within the governing administration accorded with concepts of social obligation, loyalty and service that were fundamental to the Confucian thinking that underpinned Chinese social order.[18]

China's bureaucracy was comprised of members of the literati — men educated in the classics and dedicated to Confucian ideals and values. For the majority of the hopeful candidates who sat for the entry examination, a career in the Chinese bureaucracy was their only avenue to attain political power, attract social prestige and amass a fortune. Bureaucratic appointment could be highly lucrative, with opportunities for influential postings and promotion — and success in the civil service was the only standard for success that counted in Chinese society.[19]

Attributed to **Unkoku Tōgan** Japan 1547–1618
West Lake early 17th century
Ink, light colours and gold wash on paper
Pair of six-panel screens; each screen 152.7 x 349cm
Collection: Kanazawa Nakamura Memorial Museum

The Confucian ideals that were the bedrock of the Chinese civil service recognised poetry as a highly honourable pursuit for the scholar–official — it was a compulsory component of the civil service examination and so an essential element of any ambitious young man's education. However, despite the special status with which poetry was privileged, and no matter how lauded a poet's abilities or how wide his fame, his status in society and his very identity were defined not by the quality of his verse but by his rank within the civil service.[20]

We do not know why Li Bai, a man whose obvious early genius led him to be distinguished from his peers as a 'banished immortal',[21] chose not to sit the entry examination. A fear of not finishing first in his group has been suggested,[22] and perhaps of not passing at all — many thousands failed on their first, second and even third attempts, including some of China's most renowned poets.[23] Whatever the reason, Li Bai's temperament would appear to have been ill suited to the formal etiquette of the court or the disciplined life of a political functionary. According to the *Old Book of Tang*,[24] he possessed 'a great and tameless spirit, and fantastical ways of the transcendent mind'.[25] He was fascinated by Daoism's mysticism and its advocacy of individual freedom, non-action and withdrawal.[26] These interests were tempered by his passion for more earthly pastimes: Li Bai was also an enthusiast for the pleasures of the tavern. His drinking was legendary and the delight he took in the company of dancing girls and his fellow carousers was frequently recorded in his poetry.

Li Bai's reluctance to become permanently involved in China's political administration[27] may also be explained by the fact that participation in the civil service was not without its dangers. Virtuous officials were those who felt compelled to voice concerns about affairs of state, even when such opinions were at odds with the emperor's own outlook — clearly a highly hazardous situation which required more delicate skills in tact and diplomacy than the 'tameless' Li Bai probably possessed. The perils of political office are evidenced by the sad fate of his friend, the esteemed calligrapher and Governor of Beihai Li Yong (678–747), who was unfairly accused of being involved in a plot to dethrone the Emperor and executed. Writing some years after Li Yong's death, Li Bai lamented:

> . . . what became of him? . . . When I was young
> I soon made up my mind to keep aloof from
> the world; and with his example before me
> I am less than ever tempted to win fame
> by a public career.[28]

Lin Bu was an altogether quieter personality than Li Bai, content to live in modest retirement on the West Lake, a region which boasted spectacular scenery popular with Chinese and Japanese landscape painters. A set of screens in the Kanazawa Nakamura Memorial Museum attributed to Tōeki's father Tōgan (but perhaps brushed by Tōeki and others) is a typical example of Japanese imagined views of the Lake (it is unlikely that either Tōgan or Tōeki actually visited there) which includes the pavilions and pagodas, causeways and willow trees that were ubiquitous features of West Lake views.[29]

Lin Bu added considerably to the natural charms of the location by planting hundreds of flowering plum trees around his home, creating an idyllic retreat which he apparently saw little reason to leave. Lin Bu was said to have not stepped foot in the nearby city of Hangzhou for at least 20 years. Instead, he devoted his days to tending his beloved plum trees and raising cranes — interests which led to the frequently quoted observation that Lin Bu had taken a 'plum wife and crane son' — and engaging in high-minded scholarly pursuits such as brushing calligraphy and composing poetry.[30]

Having chosen from the outset of their careers not to serve the Chinese bureaucracy, Li Bai and Lin Bu followed very different paths in life. However, their shared failure to seek official office, their apparent disregard for the status that such office would have accorded them, and their decision to instead pursue their own interests outside the bureaucracy qualified both of them to be considered as recluses. Although Lin Bu was clearly an exemplary scholar–recluse, Li Bai was not the quietly contemplative figure that we might associate with the idea of reclusion. The concept of withdrawal allowed by Confucian ethics, however, gave considerable latitude to how one chose to withdraw, how far one withdrew, and how seriously one engaged in cultivated scholarly pursuits whilst in retreat. A decisive factor in defining someone as a Confucian recluse was their rejection of official office.[31]

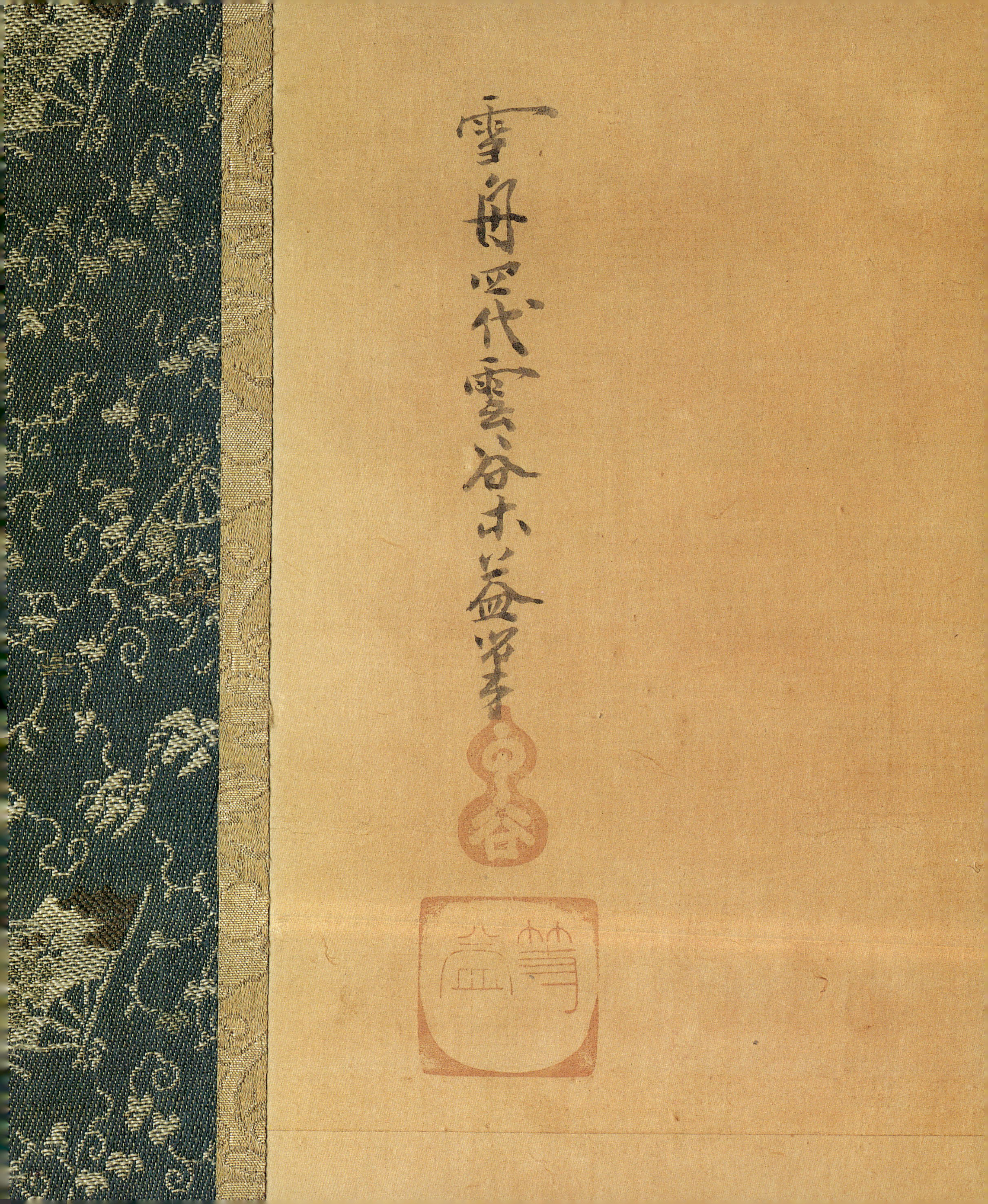
雪舟四代雲谷等益筆

Reclusion and its visual markers

Unkoku Tōeki
Landscapes with Li Bai and Lin Bu (detail: signature, left-hand screen)
c.1610–44 (early Edo period)

It is not merely the biographies of the poets that suggest that Tōeki was addressing the theme of scholarly reclusion in the Gallery's screens. In his comprehensive study of images of withdrawal in Momoyama painting, Kendall Brown has identified five recurring characteristics of Japanese treatments of the subject which are detectable in the Gallery's screens: 'communitas, scholarly pastimes, appreciation of nature, ritual poverty manifest as elegant rusticity, and reference to the Chinese past'.[32]

A subject matter and stylistic approach that referenced Chinese cultural history gave Japanese paintings the 'authority of classical precedent'.[33] Chinese culture had long been privileged with a special status in Japan, inspiring a broad-scale emulation of mainland social and cultural practices that were transformed in their new context.[34] Certainly, the Chinese past is conjured in Tōeki's depiction of the gently diffused landscapes of an idealised and imagined Lushan and West Lake — a 'Japanese dreamscape of China' as Brown describes such views — peopled with recognisable figures gleaned from China's literary past.[35] The 'Chineseness' of the subject matter is reinforced by the style in which it is depicted. From the existing works which take scholar–recluses as their subject, it is clear that Japanese artists deemed Chinese-style ink painting, either in monochrome or with a limited palette, the most appropriate medium for such high-minded themes. It was typically employed by artists of the Unkoku School for whom Chinese scholar–recluses remained favoured motifs well into the seventeenth century.[36]

Unkoku Tōgan Japan 1547–1618
Seven Sages (detail) c. late 16th or early 17th century
Ink and light colour on paper
Pair of six-panel screens; each screen 156.3 x 359.6cm
Collection: Eisei Bunko, Tokyo

The setting of the Gallery's screens is typical of Japanese paintings of scholarly reclusion. These generally place the recluse within remote mountainous landscapes in which the only sign of human habitation is a simple pavilion or hut. In the Gallery's screens, Lin Bu's spartan dwelling contrasts with the more grandiose and elaborate structures in many of the Unkoku School landscape paintings in which reclusion is not a central theme.[37] In making Lin Bu's hut the focus of the left-hand screen, Tōeki drew on the Japanese *shosaizu* tradition which takes the ideal scholar's studio as its subject. Images of such studios typically reflect a close connection to nature through their exaggerated openness and unfettered views to the landscape.[38] Indeed, Tōeki took this to an extreme by depicting holes in the roof of the hut through which Lin Bu's beloved plum blossoms may be glimpsed, subtly celebrating the refined poverty of those recluses who eschewed fame, fortune and, apparently, domestic comfort.[39]

Within Lin Bu's hut we find items associated with various scholarly pursuits. Books which allude to a scholar's learning are stacked on the table and the floor. Before him is a porcelain vase placed ready to hold the branch of plum blossom fetched by his servant, but which also references the connoisseurship and refined aesthetic sensibilities of those cultivated gentlemen who collected and appreciated such objects. A small, lidded container of the kind used to hold seal paste sits on the table. Seal paste was used to stamp the calligraphies and paintings brushed or owned by a scholar (Tōeki's own signature on the screens is stamped in this way), and containers of this type were ubiquitous items in the scholar's studio.

Also on the table is a small stack of wine cups and a wine ewer. The drinking of wine was valued for its transportative effects. By engendering a sense of abandon and spiritual and intellectual release, drunkenness allowed the scholar to travel to another realm of thought, mirroring reclusion's physical withdrawal and awakening the mind to creative and mystical inspiration. Li Bai, in particular, was famed for his love of wine[40]. On those few occasions when he held a bureaucratic position, his drinking caused some alarm within official circles: he had a reputation for being indiscreet while inebriated and it is suggested that on at least one occasion he compromised the confidentiality of some official documents which he was employed to transcribe.[41] His drunkenness was not perceived as in any way detrimental to his achievements as a poet, however, and there are countless poems penned by his admirers which celebrate Li Bai's ability to compose sublime verse while intoxicated.

Sheng Maoye China active 1594–1637
Waterfall on Mount Lu Ming Dynasty
Hanging scroll: ink and colours on silk
207 x 99.7cm
Collection: University of California, Berkeley Art Museum

The presence of several wine cups on Lin Bu's table subtly references the spirit of *communitas* or shared experience, which Brown suggests is an essential characteristic of Momoyama period depictions of scholarly reclusion.[42] The concept of withdrawal did not necessarily mean the rejection of all human contact. There is a large body of poetry and painting devoted to the subject of visiting recluses in their mountain retreats. Similarly, many Momoyama paintings depict groups of men sharing in various scholarly activities or engaging in *qing tan* (pure conversation or philosophical discussion). Some are gatherings of anonymous scholars who may reference famous figures (often one will be looking towards a waterfall in an obvious allusion to Li Bai, such as Unkoku Tōgan's screens in the Eisei Bunko Museum). Others show readily identifiable groups of Chinese scholars such as the Seven Sages of the Bamboo Grove, the Eight Immortals of the Wine Cup (which included Li Bai) or the Four Admirers (of which Lin Bu was one).[43] Groupings such as these, or pairings of individual scholars as in the Gallery's screens, emphasise a empathetic connection between like-minded individuals which frequently transcends time, as we find in the pairing of Li Bai and Lin Bu which suggests a commonality between the two men despite the fact that they lived centuries apart.[44]

The scholarly activity most obviously addressed in the Gallery's screens is Li Bai and Lin Bu's enrapt admiration for the natural world through their profound connection with the waterfall and the flowering plum. Immersion in untrammelled, unspoiled nature was a liberating and restorative alternative to the rigid constraints of both Chinese and Japanese society. It represented release, a liberation of the mind which allowed the development of self-expression.

Li Bai's love of such scenery is clearly reflected in his verse describing Lushan. Like the West Lake, Lushan was not only widely famed for its beauty but also held philosophical significance in Buddhist, Daoist and Confucian thinking and attracted many visitors. Its great popularity, however, is not evident in the Gallery's screens. Tōeki's emphasis on isolation and solitude is at odds with another contemporary view of the mountain by Sheng Maoye (active 1594–1637), which includes the pavilions, pathways and railings that were positioned for the convenience of sightseers, as well as two small groups of visitors admiring the view.[45]

Unkoku Tōgan Japan 1547–1618
Seven Sages c. late 16th or early 17th century
Ink and light colour on paper
Pair of six-panel screens; each screen 156.3 x 359.6cm
Collection: Eisei Bunko, Tokyo

Of course, Tōeki was not overly concerned with a faithful depiction of the mountain and the falls: his focus was not the waterfall at Lushan, but Li Bai's obvious appreciation of it. For Li Bai, the exhilaration he experienced at Lushan was firmly allied with his Daoist sensibilities and, certainly, his verse *Waterfall at Lu Shan* is visionary in its scope, embracing the incredible and the infinite. Vast distances, ferocious natural power, lightning and rainbows, moon and stars are all drawn upon to transform the cascade into a conduit between the mundane human world and the divine. In contemplating the falls, Li Bai is offered a tantalising glimpse into the realm of the Daoist transcendents he so desired to join:

> Let me travel to those Glorious Peaks
> Where I may feel peace grow in my heart: . . .
> And enjoy there lodging that I love,
> Ever parted from the world of men!

In seeking to be 'Ever parted from the world of men', Li Bai makes his disinterest in the conventional Confucian aspiration of serving the state abundantly clear.[46] Such sentiments, however, did not preclude images of him from being imbued with Confucian values. The Daoist search for harmony with nature and personal freedom were not irreconcilable with Confucian ideals regarding service and responsibility: it was possible to conceive a landscape in which both Confucian tradition and Daoist idealism could be embraced and accommodated.[47] One example of the overlayering of Confucian symbolism on an essentially Daoist theme is the Eisei Bunko Museum screens. As Brown suggests, Tōgan's inclusion of a group of large pine trees — a plant strongly associated with the Confucian values of moral strength and political integrity — in his depiction of the Seven Sages infused Confucian values into what was otherwise an anti-Confucian theme.[48] This interpretation has some resonance for our own reading of the Gallery's screens. Following this logic, the large pine growing at the top of the falls which stretches across the abyss towards a spellbound Li Bai assists in bringing the poet within the ambit of Confucian reclusion.

Lin Bu's representation as an ideal scholar–recluse requires little clarification. His beloved plum blossoms had been a popular subject in Chinese literature and painting for many centuries. As the first plant to come into flower, even while winter snows are still on the ground, the plum has long been a potent symbol of resilience and renewal in East Asian cultures. Its delicately scented and gently blushed blossoms — harbingers of the promise of spring within a bleak and barren landscape — represent the plum's much admired strength and spirit. At the same time, its singularity as the only plant in flower at the very beginning of spring imbues the plum with a sense of isolation that associates it with idea of scholarly reclusion.[49]

No scholar–recluse has enjoyed a closer association with the flowering plum than Lin Bu, but although his affinity with the natural world is most obviously expressed through his admiration for the plum, it may also be detected in his love for the crane. Like the plum, the crane enjoyed a long history of symbolic significance in both China and Japan. It was considered an auspicious emblem of longevity, vitality, purity and propitiousness, and as a messenger of wisdom, its call represented the voices of men of virtue and talent which could be heard by a wise ruler.[50]

Unkoku Tōgan Japan 1547–1618
Landscapes with Tao Yuanming and Lin Heijing (detail)
1547–1618 (Momoyama period)
Ink and gold wash on paper
Pair of six-panel screens; each screen 147 x 358cm
Collection: The Asian Art Museum of San Francisco.
The Avery Brundage Collection

Lin Bu's empathetic connection with the crane is perhaps more evident in a pair of screens painted by Tōgan, now in the Asian Art Museum of San Francisco, in which his attention is taken not by the nearby plum, but by a returning crane. The presence of a crane draws heavily on the idea that Lin Bu's moral purity allowed him to develop a special bond with the birds. The crane's symbolic freedom, virtue and propriety made it an ideal companion for a scholar–recluse and a single crane was often used to symbolise the scholar's harmony with the natural world or even to signify the scholar himself.[51] In the Gallery's screens, the presence of a single crane serves a dual purpose: not only did Tōeki thoughtfully pair the symbolism of the plum and crane to enable us to identify Lin Bu, but the lone crane underscores the theme of both screens as being one of high-minded scholarly reclusion.

Unkoku Tōeki
Landscapes with Li Bai and Lin Bu (detail: left-hand screen) c.1610–44 (early Edo period)

Unkoku Tōeki Japan 1591–1644
Landscapes with Li Bai and Lin Bu c.1610–44 (early Edo period)
Ink, colours and gold wash on paper on six-fold wooden framed screens (*byobu*), edged with woven silk and covered verso in paper relief printed in black
Pair of six-panel screens; 169 x 377.2cm (overall comp.)
Gift of James Fairfax, AO, through the Queensland Art Gallery Foundation 1992
Collection: Queensland Art Gallery

The Power of Reclusion

Unkoku Tōeki
Landscapes with Li Bai and Lin Bu (detail: right-hand screen) c.1610–44 (early Edo period)

Scholarly reclusion had been a popular theme in Japanese literature and painting long before Tōeki painted the Gallery's screens. With the introduction of Buddhism to Japan in the sixth century, withdrawal became associated with religious detachment, and Zen principles and practices in particular had a profound influence on the literature, philosophy and artistic expression of reclusion in Japan. By the Momoyama and early Edo periods, however, images of withdrawal became imbued with political significance.[52]

Since the twelfth century, Japan had embraced a political structure in which real power — that of military and economic control — was vested not in the emperor and the court but in the *bushi* or warrior class. Supreme political authority lay with the shogun, the most powerful of Japan's daimyo (warlords) whose dominance was made possible by the consensus of the lesser daimyo. While the emperor maintained his sovereignty, his role was essentially ceremonial and symbolic. He was responsible for safeguarding Japan's cultural traditions and granting official titles and ranks including that of shogun.

By the mid fifteenth century, the shogun's power had considerably diminished. Over the course of the next 100 years (a period known as Sengoku Jidai, the 'Age of the Country at War') Japan lacked any semblance of a strong central authority and the country faced extreme political fragmentation. Beyond the immediate confines of Kyoto, the power of an exhausted and impotent shogunate barely impacted. Daimyo became autonomous powers within their own territories, their energies devoted to increasing, consolidating or defending their local pre-eminence. It was a period in which warfare was endemic. There was a rapid turnover of authority as great military houses rose and fell and new daimyo emerged. Alliances were readily made and broken. Daimyo battled with daimyo, vassal samurai rose against their masters, and peasant rebellion was frequent and brutally suppressed.

The mid sixteenth-century emergence of three capable leaders who shared a vision for a strong, reunified Japan marked a pivotal moment in Japanese history. Over the next 50 years, the bloody and brutal ascendancy of Oda Nobunaga (1534–82), his brilliant general and successor Toyotomi Hideyoshi (1536–98), and the powerful and politically astute Tokugawa Ieyasu (1543–1616), brought an increasing number of daimyo and their territories under their sway. Thanks to their outstanding ability as military strategists, their forging of judicious alliances and, in Nobunaga's case, the targeting and undermining of the Buddhist monasteries whose power threatened his own, this period of consolidation was finally brought to a close with the establishment in 1603 of the Tokugawa shogunate which would dominate a unified Japan for the next two-and-a-half centuries.

Images of reclusion were most effective as carriers of political meaning during periods of disorder. Scenes of withdrawal into a peaceful and benign natural realm far from the concerns and responsibilities of political office, the brutality of warfare and the strictures of an intensely observed social hierarchy must have offered their viewers a welcome respite. It is little wonder that in the Momoyama and early Edo periods (an era of unprecedented political unrest and transformation), the theme of scholarly reclusion was adopted with such enthusiasm by Japanese artists and their patrons. [53]

What is remarkable about the way scholarly reclusion was conceived in the Momoyama and early Edo period, though, is its multivalency. Images addressing the theme are known to have been in the possession of Buddhist monasteries, members of the aristocracy and Japan's military elite, and while the aspirations for, connections with and ability to exercise real political power for each of these patron groups varied widely, the symbolism of the recluse could accommodate them all.[54]

That the theme had a resonance for each of these groups suggests the existence of a shared symbolism based around the recluse which, despite the differences in their circumstances, the aristocracy, the priesthood and the military elite were all able to draw on for their own ends.[55] As a result, images of the scholar–recluse could be used to endorse two diametrically opposed points of view. On the one hand, when approached from the perspective of the politically powerful military elite, the theme could legitimise the exercise of power. It suggested an intellectual affiliation with the scholar–recluse whose interests lay not in the mundane world of political affairs but with more high-minded pursuits — a rejection which paradoxically made the erudite, incorruptible recluse the ideal figure to wield political power.[56] Alternatively, for the court and the aristocracy who were becoming increasingly marginalised, and for the priesthood whose influence had been severely curtailed during the process of reunification and by the escalating secularisation of Japanese society,[57] scholarly reclusion could express a desire for detachment that represented a criticism or rejection of the prevailing political order.[58]

Reclusion in the service of power

Unkoku Tōeki
Landscapes with Li Bai and Lin Bu (detail: left-hand screen) c.1610–44 (early Edo period)

Although it was brute force that had allowed many daimyo to gain ascendancy during the period leading up to Tokugawa rule, they also maintained their authority and social prestige by less bloody means. In such uncertain times, daimyo were keen to assert their legitimacy through any avenue available to them, military and civilian. They found an appropriate and peaceful means to express their authority in the concept of *kōgi* or 'the public good', which required daimyo to make public assertions of their ethical conduct, administrative ability and cultural sophistication.[59] Daimyo culture became increasingly characterised by a synthesis of the traditions of the warrior (*bu*) and the abilities and interests of the scholar (*bun*), neatly encapsulated by the aphorism, 'brush and sword in accord'.[60] As a consequence, the Momoyama and early Edo periods saw daimyo emerge as Japan's dominant cultural as well as political force.

For the skills associated with *bun* to be effective as tools of legitimation, it was crucial that a daimyo not only possessed the cultural learning of a scholar but that he was seen to do so. The demonstration of a refined aesthetic sensibility provided tangible proof of a daimyo's superior abilities (as well as making manifest his wealth and prestige) and conferred on him a cultural authority that translated into political legitimacy. This was readily expressed by the types of objects he collected and the methods adopted for their display within the formal audience halls of a daimyo's castle.

Naturally, daimyo of the Momoyama and early Edo periods, while establishing their own aesthetic standards in their patronage of favoured artists and artisans, also turned to established patterns of acquisition and display in order to stamp their collections with the authority of tradition. The taste in objects collected for exhibition at official functions held within the audience halls or used in the daily life of the daimyo and his family had been established and codified during the Ashikaga shogunate (1336–1573), and it was Ashikaga tastes that the daimyo of following centuries sought to emulate in order to prove their own erudition and refinement.[61]

Japan
Arrangements for reception room display (Zashiki kazari emaki)
(detail) 1522 (Muromachi Period) (copied 1559)
Handscroll: ink and colour on paper
28.4 x 575cm
Private collection, Japan

The Ashikaga had employed specialist advisors known as *go-kaisho no dōbōshū* (guest-hall companions) in the role of cultural guides charged with the responsibility of curating and cataloguing the shogunal art collections, and the records they left continued to be the principle reference works on the subject into the Edo period.[62] These were avidly studied by daimyo to ensure that their own collections conformed with the accepted conventions and give us some idea of the types of objects considered appropriate for public display. These included ink paintings, fine ceramics, and superb lacquerwares with a marked preference for things Chinese. The cachet of Chinese culture remained an important factor in Japanese aesthetic tastes and ink painting with Chinese styles and subjects — such as the Gallery's screens — were particularly favoured for display in rooms used for official functions.[63]

For daimyo who were keen to assert their cultural superiority, screens such as those in the Gallery's collection held an obvious appeal. Brushed by an artist belonging to an important and highly regarded Japanese School, the screens would have communicated their owner's sophisticated aesthetic sensibilities. By drawing on Chinese models of depiction and subject matter in their illustration of two eminent poets, the screens would have established their owner's intellectual authority. But most importantly, the deeper meaning of the screens — their focus on the concept of reclusion — demonstrated their owner's claim to legitimacy and ethical standing through his scholarly knowledge and conduct, even if they did so only symbolically.[64]

Although the Confucian ethics which informed Japanese political administration obviously placed great emphasis on the principle of contributing to and participating in government, the ideals associated with reclusion were widely admired. A scholar–recluse's disinterest in the accumulation of the wealth and power that were the rewards of engagement in official public life was the ultimate expression of Confucian piety and a highly beneficial panacea for the ambition and self interest that so frequently informed the seeking and holding of political office.[65]

China
Mallet shaped vase 960–1127 (Song dynasty)
Celadon
26.5cm (h.)
Collection: James Fairfax, AO
Photograph: Brenton McGeachie

This reading of reclusion had particular appeal for those ambitious men in positions of power who were keen to use the idea, although not the practice, of scholarly reclusion to demonstrate their own fitness to rule. For these men real reclusion was an impossibility, yet they were able to benefit from the concept by associating themselves with the ideals of the scholar–recluse through their ownership and display of imagery such as the Gallery's screens. This is particularly true for those screens which were used as backdrops for a figure of authority, and such an association is emphasised by the pictorial arrangement of the Gallery's screens. Here the two Chinese poets are depicted within expanded foregrounds to the far right and left, which are framed by natural features such as rocks and trees — a typical composition for Japanese paintings of figures within a landscape.[66] The centre of the screens dissolves to a more distant view that could accommodate the presence of the patron–owner. The poets themselves turn to face the centre so that their attention might be as much engaged by the natural authority of the man seated before them as by the natural beauty of the waterfall and plum blossom.

Reclusion and the rejection of power

Unkoku Tōeki
Landscapes with Li Bai and Lin Bu (detail: right-hand screen) c.1610–44 (early Edo period)

Affiliating oneself with the idea of reclusion was all very well, but permanent physical withdrawal would seem to have been at odds with the Confucian ideals of participation and service that had such a profound influence on the formulation of political policy in the Momoyama and early Edo periods. According to neo-Confucian ethics, however, there were some circumstances in which real, physical withdrawal was acceptable.[67]

Early Confucianism accommodated the concept of reclusion within its philosophy, justifying withdrawal by suggesting that when a ruler was corrupt and immoral or the official's own principles were threatened with compromise, withdrawal was both necessary and commendable.[68] The criteria determining an official's decision to withdraw or not was his own moral judgment and ethical values.[69]

This sympathetic stance fell out of favour as the idea of service to society became the imperative, no matter what the attitudes or actions of the ruler. While criticism of the ruler was acceptable and indeed an official's duty (although very cautiously voiced), their loyalty to him had to remain unwavering, whether or not he chose to accept or act upon their remonstrances.[70] The increasing emphasis laid by neo-Confucian ideology on the concept of loyalty to one's ruler meant that those who refused to serve the state were perceived as morally dubious. But the concept of a steadfast and unswerving loyalty also meant that it was considered to survive the demise of dynasty. While an official who chose not to serve the state under normal conditions was treated with suspicion, those who chose to continue in office and serve a new dynasty were vilified as ethically untenable.[71]

In Japan, those who had not fared well in the political and martial machinations of the period, or who found warfare and intrigue not to their taste, must have found images of withdrawal highly appealing. The scrabble for local dominance that characterised the Sengoku period, and the shifts in power that marked the process of reunification and the eventual establishment of the Tokugawa shogunate, meant that for every daimyo who gained ascendancy, there were many whose political power and influence were severely curtailed.

For those daimyo and their retainers for whom a removal from power had been enforced, and for a disenfranchised aristocracy and Buddhist priesthood, the neo-Confucian interpretation of an ethically grounded reclusion must have offered some comfort. The symbolism of the scholar–recluse, while adopted by those in power to endorse the legitimacy of their political authority, also allowed scope for a subtle criticism of that authority.

Read from this perspective, the Gallery's screens provided a delicately understated counter-ideology. It was one that implied that those who associated themselves with images of withdrawal were not only more interested in the enlightened and erudite pursuits of the scholar–recluse than in the cut and thrust of political life, but that they preferred withdrawal from society rather than compromise their loyalties and ethical ideals by serving a new political authority to which they were morally opposed. Images of scholarly reclusion and the high-minded principles they represented helped make the bitter taste of defeat more palatable. The idea of reclusion afforded those who were now removed from power the opportunity to throw a favourable light on their diminished status by emphasising their moral virtue.[72] At the very least, it allowed them to effect an air of lofty indifference.

This begs the question of why imagery such as this, which contained implicit censure, was tolerated by those in power who otherwise maintained such a tight control on Japanese society. One explanation is that scholarly reclusion as it was conceived in the painting of the period provided a 'necessary safety valve in a society where silent acquiescence was the rule'.[73]

In essence, images of scholarly reclusion provided the opportunity for the safe expression of dangerous ideas. As highly idealised and aestheticised representations of men living in benign and beautiful landscapes and engaged in erudite activities, images of reclusion hardly jeopardised social or political stability in any real sense but, rather, served as a subtle reminder of moral and social values, their criticisms 'implicit rather than explicit and, essentially, constructive rather [than] destructive'.[74] Even when critical of the prevailing political power, the concept of scholarly reclusion and its depiction in imagery such as the Gallery's screens assisted in preserving the social order. It provided a relatively harmless outlet through which a disaffected citizenry could channel feelings of disappointment and disenfranchisement.[75]

Sarah Tiffin
Curator, Historical Asian Art, Queensland Art Gallery

ENDNOTES

1 Trans. Shigeyoshi Obata, *The Works of Li Po the Chinese Poet*, Paragon Book Reprint Corp., New York, 1965, p.20; first published in 1935.

2 Sometimes written Li Po or Li Bo; also known as Taibai and Qinglian Jushi and as Ritaihaku or Rihaku and Shouren Koji in Japan.

3 Sometimes written Lin Pu; also known as Lin Hejing and as Rin Pu or Rinnasei in Japan. I am grateful to Timothy Clark, Head of the Japanese Section of the Department of Asia at the British Museum, and Yamamoto Hideo, Curator of Painting at the Kyoto National Museum, for their assistance in confirming the identities of the figures in the screens.

4 Sesshū's own painting style was developed by copying Chinese paintings of the Song (960–1279) and Yuan (1279–1368) periods which had been exported to Japan, and also through his exposure to the work of contemporary Ming (1368–1644) artists during his travels in China in 1467–69.

5 Tōgan had been charged by his patrons, the Mōri (a powerful daimyo or warlord family based in western Japan), with the task of copying a landscape handscroll by Sesshū which was a Mōri family treasure. They were so pleased with his efforts that they gave him the use of Sesshū's former studio–residence *Unkoku-an* in Suō province (now Yamaguchi Prefecture), from which the School's name derived. He assumed the name Tōgan (his former name was Hara Jihei) using the character 'tō' adopted from Sesshū's name Tōyō (a character which also appears in Tōeki's name and those of many other members of the Unkoku School), and was granted permission to claim succession from Sesshū. It is thought that Tōgan also studied the techniques of the Kanō School in the early stages of his career.

6 Yamamoto Hideo, *Unkokuha no Keifu*, Yamaguchi Prefectural Museum of Art, Yamaguchi, 1986, p.158.

7 Barbara Brennan Ford and Oliver R. Impey, *Japanese Art from the Gerry Collection in the Metropolitan Museum of Art*, Metropolitan Museum of Art, New York, 1989, p.23; and Robert D. Jacobsen, *The Art of Japanese Screen Painting: Selections from the Minneapolis Institute of Arts*, Minneapolis Institute of Arts, Minneapolis, 1984, p.7.

8 Wu Hung, *The Double screen: Medium and Representation in Chinese Painting*, Reaktion Books, London, 1996, p.13. See also Kendall H. Brown, *The Politics of Reclusion: Painting and Power in Momoyama Japan*, University of Hawaii Press, Honolulu, 1997, pp.14–15, regarding the construction of a 'metaphoric world' by *shōhekiga* (wall painting) and *fusuma* (sliding screens).

9 See Wu Hung p.12 and p.14 regarding representations and descriptions of Chinese court ceremonies.

10 Wu Hung, p.134. This is an approach also adopted by Kendall Brown.

11 *The Complete Poems of the Tang Dynasty (Quan Tang shi)* is an anthology of some 48 900 poems by 2300 poets and, as it was compiled many centuries after the dynasty's demise, it must include only a fraction of what was actually written. (Obata, p.1.)

12 Arthur Cooper (ed. and trans.), *Li Po and Tu Fu*, Penguin, Harmondsworth, 1973, p.158. The poem also exists in a shorter format which focuses on the imagery of the first verse.

13 Maggie Bickford et al, *Bones of Jade, Soul of Ice: The Flowering Plum in Chinese Art*, Yale University Art Gallery, New Haven, 1985, p.24. See also Maggie Bickford, *Ink Plum: The Making of a Chinese Scholar-Painting Genre*, Cambridge University Press, Cambridge, 1996, p.23. The full poem reads:

When other fragrant plants have withered, it alone is lovely,
It holds a monopoly on charm in the small garden.
Its sparse shadows are horizontal and slanted — the water is clear and shallow;
Its hidden fragrance wafts and moves — the moon is hazy and dim.
A frosty bird, about to alight, first eyes the tree stealthily;
A powdered butterfly, if it could know it, would be spellbound.
Luckily I have a little song with which to approach it,
No need for the beat of sandalwood clappers or shared drinks in golden cups.

(Bickford, *Bones of Jade, Soul of Ice*, p.165.)

14 See, for example, the work of Ouyang Xiu (1007–72), whose critiques and commentaries had a profound influence on Song literary tastes. He wrote of Lin Bu's couplet 'there certainly were many who wrote poems on the flowering plum in past generations, but never before such lines as these!' (Bickford, *Ink Plum*, pp.23–24, quoting from Ouyang Xiu's *Guitian lu (Record of Returning to the Fields)*. See also Bickford, *Bones of Jade, Soul of Ice*, p.24.)

15 Bickford, *Bones of Jade, Soul of Ice*, n.2, p.165.

16 For example, the paintings of Zhongren (d.1123), the foremost practitioner of the *momei* or plum ink painting, were frequently associated with Lin Bu's poetry. See, for example, commentaries on Zhongren's painting by Song Lian (1320–81), Huang Tingjian (1045–1105), Huihong (1071–1128), and Liu Kezhuang (1187–1269). Inscriptions dating from the Song dynasty added to Zhongren's *momei* also frequently reference the Lin Bu or his couplet. (Bickford, *Ink Plum*, p.115 and pp.125–26.)

17 Bickford, *Ink Plum*, p.24.

18 Confucianism is the system of social, ethical, political and philosophical thought based on the teachings of Kongzi (c.551–471BCE; also known as Kong Fu Zi or Confucius) and his followers. Kongzi's teachings, as recorded at least a century after his death in *The Analects*, stress the importance of establishing good government through the cultivation of proper, moral conduct by individuals and the development of a correct and stable social organisation. Although his teachings were not accepted during his own lifetime, Confucianism became the state orthodoxy during the Han dynasty and, despite Buddhism and Daoism becoming highly influential at various stages in China's history, Confucianism remained the seminal influence on Chinese political and social thinking.

19 Winston W. Lo, *An Introduction to the Civil Service of Sung China*, University of Hawaii Press, Honolulu, 1987, p.25.

20 A. R. Davis (ed.), and Robert Kotewall and Norman L. Smith (trans.), *The Penguin Book of Chinese Verse*, Penguin Books, Harmondsworth, 1962, p.lviii; and Arthur Waley, *The Poetry and Career of Li Po, 701–762 A.D.*, Allen and Unwin, London, 1950, p.99.

21 This term, originally used to describe someone of vastly superior talent, was often used from the time of Song dynasty to refer specifically to Li Bai. (Alfreda Murck, *Poetry and Painting in Song China: The Subtle Art of Dissent*, Harvard University Asia Center, Cambridge, 2000, p.140.)

22 Cooper, p. 28.

23 For example, Li Bai's friend and contemporary Du Fu (712–70; sometimes written Tu Fu; also known as also known as Du Shaoling and Du Gongbu), considered one of the few poets to rival Li Bai's poetic abilities. He was unsuccessful on two occasions and only gained entry by sitting a 'special examination' after coming to the Emperor's notice, but he was disappointed in the position eventually offered to him.

24 The *Old Book of Tang or Jiu Tang shu* is one of the official dynastic histories of China, compiled by Liu Xu (887–946) in the mid tenth century.

25 Obata, p.19.

26 Daoism is the philosophical system traditionally founded by Lao Zi (c. fourth century BCE; sometimes written Laozi, Lao Tse or Lao Tzu). Dao or 'the Way' is the governing principle or essence of the universe which is considered to be in a constant state of flux. In contrast to early Confucian orthodoxy, Daoism embraces the metaphysical, emphasising that personal freedom, inaction, spontaneity, and harmony with the natural environment will ensure the development of correct behaviour and a proper social order. Daoism also incorporates more esoteric practices and beliefs including an interest in alchemy, immortality and mysticism.

27 Li Bai did, on occasion, hold official positions that were granted to him in recognition of his poetic prowess, but none of these were particularly successful or long lasting. In 742 he was invited to appear at court and, after impressing the emperor with his verse, was awarded a place at the elite Hanlin Academy. He was unable to turn this notice to his long-term advantage, however, and in 744 he was forced to leave.

28 Waley, p.50–51. In later life, however, Li Bai seems to have had a change of heart. After the lifting of his sentence of exile, his verse took on a somewhat aggrieved tone in which he expressed a wish to regain the favour of the court and fulfil the conformist Confucian ambition to be of service to the state. During this period, he spent some time living on the northern edge of Dongting Lake in the XiaoXiang region of southern China, an area which for some centuries had been associated with an imposed and often unjust political exile. (Murck, p. 6.) Such associations colour Li Bai's richly allegorical verses of this period in which he bemoans his fate as a neglected man of unrecognised political genius. (See, for example, Murck's analysis of Li Bai's *Distant Separation* (Murck, p. 22).)

29 Bruce A. Coats [catalogue entry], in Money L. Hickman et al, *Japan's Golden Age: Momoyama*, Yale University Press, New Haven, 1996, p.168.

30 Bickford, *Ink Plum*, p.23.

31 Frederick W. Mote, 'Confucian Eremitism in the Yüan period', in Arthur F. Wright (ed.) *The Confucian Persuasion*, Stanford University Press, Stanford, 1960, pp.203–04. The latitude afforded the notion of withdrawal, however, allowed reclusion to be a mental as much as a physical state. There were many scholars who considered themselves recluses, even while actively engaged in political service, by cultivating a reclusive state of mind and enacting withdrawal in their garden retreats or scholar's studios. This attitude towards reclusion was also adopted in Japan.

32 Brown, p.11.

33 Brown, p.104.

34 The impact of Chinese culture is traceable from Japan's earliest written records and although from time to time contact with continental Asia was restricted, it was never completely severed. Although the Heian period (794–1185) marked a resurgence in Japanese tastes and aesthetics, Chinese influence was reasserted from the Muromachi period (1338–1568) with a renewed interest in the adoption and adaptation of Chinese cultural practices that remained strong amongst Japan's political elite into the Edo period.

35 Brown, p.13.

36 Brown, p.103 and p.105.

37 Brown, p.12 and p.94–97.

38 Brown, p.96.

39 Here Tōeki has used the same motif employed by the twelfth century Japanese poet–recluse Ryōzen in his verse *Composed When Moonlight Was Shining Through the Openings of My Dilapidated Hut*:

I have even seen
The moonlight as it filtered
through the roof planks —
A hut that verges on collapse
Provides the finest place to live.

(trans. Mezaki Tokue, 'Aesthete-Recluses During the Transition from Ancient to Medieval Japan', in Earl Miner (ed.), *Principles of Classical Japanese Literature*, Princeton University Press, Princeton, 1985, p.165.)

40 J. Keith Wilson, 'The fine art of drinking: The Chinese silversmith Zhu Bishan and his sculptural cups', in *Bulletin of Cleveland Museum of Art*, vol.81, no.10, December 1994, p.392.

41 Waley, p.25.

42 Brown, p.83ff.

43 The Seven Sages of the Bamboo Grove were a group of scholars, poets and musicians who escaped the political chaos of the transition to the Jin dynasty to live in reclusion in a bamboo grove. They are: Ruan Ji (210–63), Ji Kang (223–66), Shan Tao (205–66); Xiang Xiu (221–300), Liu Ling (c.225–80), Wang Rong (234–305), and Ruan Xian (third century). The Eight Immortals of the Wine Cup were Tang poets who were prodigious drinkers, grouped together by Du Fu in his poem of the same name. They are: Li Bai, He Zhizhang, Wang Jin, Li Shizhi, Cui Zongzhi, Su Jin, Zhang Xu and Jiao Sui. The Four Admirers are a group of four scholars famed for their love of particular flowers. They are: Lin Bu (plum), Tao Yuanming (chrysanthemum), Huang Shangu (orchid), and Zhou Maoshu (lotus).

44 Davis, p.lx.; and Brown, p.98–99.

45 See Burkus-Chasson for her comparison of Shitao's *Waterfall on Mount Lu* and this work. (Anne Burkus-Chasson, '"Clouds and Mists That Emanate and Sink Away": Shitao's Waterfall on Mount Lu and practices of observation in the seventeenth century', in *Art History*, vol.19, no.2, June 1996, p.173.) This absence is also evident in the Gallery's Lin Bu screen. The isolated setting is in stark contrast to the obviously populated view of the West Lake seen in the pair of screens attributed to Tōgan but possibly brushed by Tōeki.

46 This is an interpretation that Burkus-Chasson similarly applies to *Lu Mountain Ballad*. (Burkus-Chasson, p.176ff.)

47 Ford and Impey, p.30.

48 Brown, p.94.

49 The beauty of plum blossoms, however, is only fleeting as they are not long lasting, something which has also associated the flowering plum with transience, particularly with regard to feminine beauty. The plum, then, as a symbol both of resilience and of transience evoked mixed emotions. As Maggie Bickford has noted, the annual arrival of the plum blossom was greeted with a 'spirit of tender ambivalence, embracing pleasure and regret'. (Bickford, *Bones of Jade, Soul of Ice*, p.18.)

50 Houmei Song, 'Images of the crane in Chinese painting', in *Oriental Art*, Autumn 1998, p.14.

51 Richard M. Barnhart, *Peach Blossom Spring: Gardens and Flowers in Chinese Paintings*, Metropolitan Museum of Art, New York, 1983, p.132.

52 This aspect of reclusion is explored at length in Brown's study of scholarly reclusion in Japanese painting of the Momoyama period. Another publication which examines the connections between reclusion and political power in Japan is Michele Marra's *The Aesthetics of Discontent: Politics and Reclusion in Medieval Japanese Literature*, University of Hawaii Press, Honolulu, 1991.

53 Brown, p.176 and p.13.

54 Brown, p.13 and p.171.

55 Brown, p.10–11, p.13–14 and p.171.

56 Brown, p.60.

57 As Bito Masahide has observed, '[t]he Early Modern period was . . . an age of secularisation and scant religious feeling . . . The regular annual observances of Buddhism lost their character as expression[s] of religious faith and there was a pronounced tendency to turn them into mere customary ceremony'. (Bito Masahide, 'Society and economy in the Edo Period', in William Watson (ed.), *The Great Japan Exhibition: Art of the Edo Period 1600–1868*, Royal Academy of Arts, London, and Weidenfeld and Nicolson, London, 1981, p.24.)

58 Brown, p.176.

59 Brown, p.53 ff.

60 Victor Harris, 'Arms: The balance of peace', in Robert T. Singer et al, *Edo: Art in Japan 1615–1868*, National Gallery of Art, Washington, 1999, p.109. Similarly, Hayashi Razan (1583–1657), an advisor to Tokugawa Ieyasu, declared 'How can a man discharge the duties of his rank and position without combining the peaceful and military arts?' (Christine Guth, 'The Tokugawa as patrons and collectors of painting', in *The Japan of the Shoguns: The Tokugawa Collection*, Montreal Museum of Fine Arts, Montreal, 1989, p.43, citing the *Hayashi Razan bunshō*.)

61 Yoshinobu Tokugawa, 'A Daimyo's possessions', in *The Shogun Age Exhibition*, Shogun Age Exhibition Executive Committee, Tokyo, 1983, p.29. Indeed, most Ashikaga shoguns were better known for their artistic and intellectual accomplishments than for their prowess on the battlefield. (John T. Carpenter, 'China in Japan: The Shogun's court fifteenth–sixteenth centuries', in Nicole Coolidge Rousamiere (ed.) *Arts of Kazari: Japan on Display*, British Museum Press, London, 2002, p.86.)

62 Kawai Masatomo, 'Reception room display in mediaeval Japan', in *Arts of Kazari: Japan on Display*, ed. Nicole Coolidge Rousamiere, British Museum Press, London, 2002, p.39ff. The most celebrated and influential of the Ashikaga guest-hall companions were the father, son and grandson Nōami (1397–1494), Geiōami (1431–85),and Sōami (d. 1525), collectively known as the San'ami (three Ami), who served the shoguns Yoshinori (1394–1441) and Yoshimasa (1436–90). The records they left were Sōami's *Zashiki kazari shidai* (*Arrangements for Reception Room Display*, c.1511) and *O-kazari sho* (*Records of Display*, 1523), and the *Kundaikan sōchōki* (*Record of Arrangements in the Shogunal Guest Hall*) drafted by Nōami and later expanded by Sōami.

63 Ford and Impey, p.25.

64 Brown, p.58 and p.88–89. See also Ford and Impey, p.33; and Coats, p.153.

65 Li Chi, 'The Changing concept of the recluse in Chinese literature', in *Harvard Journal of Asiatic Studies*, vol. 24, 1962, p.245. See also *Momoyama: Japanese Art in the Age of Grandeur*, Metropolitan Museum of Art, New York, 1976, p.12–13; and Brown, p.60.

66 Ford and Impey, p.25.

67 The emergence of Neo-Confucianism during the Song dynasty marked a resurgence in the pre-eminence of Confucianism. In response to the popularity of Buddhism and Daoism during the preceding Tang dynasty, Confucian thinkers incorporated a number of metaphysical aspects into their teachings and practices, claiming a transcendent sanction or foundation for the established social order and institutions, and emphasising ascetic practices and spiritual self-cultivation.

68 Li Chi, p.238 and p.239, and Mote, p.206.

69 Mote, p.206.

70 Mote, p.230. See also Murck, p.1.

71 Mote, p.208.

72 Brown, p.176.

73 Brown, p.44–45.

74 Brown, p.45.

75 Brown, p.72 and p.175.

CATALOGUE OF WORKS

Unkoku Tōeki Japan 1591–1644
Landscapes with Li Bai and Lin Bu
c.1610–44 (early Edo period)
Ink, colours and gold wash on paper on six-fold wooden framed screens (*byobu*), edged with woven silk and covered verso in paper relief printed in black
Pair of six-panel screens;
169 x 377.2cm (overall comp.)
Gift of James Fairfax, AO, through the Queensland Art Gallery Foundation 1992
Collection: Queensland Art Gallery

Bizen kilns Japan
Narrow necked jar with lugs (tsubo)
1568–1615 (Momoyama period)
Stoneware, coil built with natural ash glaze
30.9 x 35cm (diam.)
Purchased 1994 with funds from Idemitsu Kosan Co., Ltd through the Queensland Art Gallery Foundation
Collection: Queensland Art Gallery

Tokoname kilns Japan
Narrow-necked jar (tsubo)
1392–1568 (Muromachi period)
Coil built stoneware with 'fly ash' glaze and kiln deposit
43.2 x 53.1cm (diam.)
Purchased 1992 with funds from James Fairfax, AO, through the Queensland Art Gallery Foundation
Collection: Queensland Art Gallery

China
Tea bowl
960–1127 (Song dynasty)
Stoneware, thrown flaring dark red body with 'hare's fur' glaze
6.4 x 12.4cm (diam.)
Gift of Stanley Lipscombe 1952
Collection: Queensland Art Gallery

China
Covered box decorated with lychee sprays
late 16th century (Ming dynasty)
Carved cinnabar lacquer with black lacquer interior
3.6 x 7cm
Purchased 1989
Collection: Art Gallery of New South Wales

Attributed to **Gu Jianlong** China 1606–c.86
Scholars gathering in the Western Garden
1705 (Qing dynasty)
Handscroll: ink and colour on silk
26.1 x 283cm
Purchased 1956
Collection: Art Gallery of New South Wales

Japan
Cup decorated with figure of Tao Yuanming
late 17th century – early 18th century (Edo period)
Porcelain with 'famille verte' decoration
2.7 x 7.3cm
Gift from the J.H. Myrtle Collection 2000
Collection: Art Gallery of New South Wales

Kano Tan'yu Japan 1602–1674
Mokuan Shoto, calligrapher
China/Japan 1611–1684
Sparrow on a blossoming plum tree
1661 (Edo period)
Hanging scroll: ink on paper
32.7 x 56.2 cm (image and sheet)
Purchased through The Art Foundation of Victoria with the assistance of Mr S. Baillieu Myer, AC, Founder Benefactor, 1993
Collection: National Gallery of Victoria

Korea
Tea bowl
15th century (Chōson dynasty)
Stoneware
5.9 x 14.4 cm diameter
Lillian Ernestine Lobb Bequest, 2003
Collection: National Gallery of Victoria

Japan
Tea bowl
1615–1868 (Edo period)
Earthenware (Raku ware)
8.1 x 11.9 cm diameter
Felton Bequest, 1921
Collection: National Gallery of Victoria

Japan
Dish
15th century (Muromachi period)
Lacquer on wood
3.3 x 32.8 cm (diam.)
Presented through The Art Foundation of Victoria by Mr S. Baillieu Myer, AC, Founder Benefactor, 1989
Collection: National Gallery of Victoria

Tosa Mitsunori Japan 1583–1638
The Tale of Genji
17th century (Edo period)
Album: pigments and gold paint on paper on gold painted cardboard, 56 pages, gold thread, silk and wood cover, glued binding
14.8 x 13.2 cm (image and sheet)
19.8 x 16.7 cm (page) (each)
19.8 x 16.7 x 9.2 cm (closed)
19.8 x 968.6 x 4.6 cm (open)
Purchased 1967
Collection: National Gallery of Victoria

China (Jingdezhen, Jiangxi province)
Wine ewer
1127–1279 (Southern Song dynasty)
Porcelain (Qingbai ware)
10.0 x 11.0 x 9.0 cm
Felton Bequest 1939
Collection: National Gallery of Victoria

Wang Xi China active mid 14th century
Birds and flowering plants
mid 14th century (Yuan dynasty)
Hanging scroll: ink, pigments on silk
106.3 x 55.2 cm (image and sheet)
Purchased 1999
Collection: National Gallery of Victoria

Japan
Table
late 18th – early 19th century (Edo period)
Nashiji and hiramaki-e lacquer
28 x 38cm (diam.)
Collection: James Fairfax, AO

Suzuki Kiitsu Japan 1796–1858
Table screen depicting Autumn plants
early 19th century (Edo period)
Ink and colours on silk
42 x 88cm
Collection: James Fairfax, AO

Japan
No bento
1615–1868 (Edo period)
Nashiji and hiramaki-e lacquer
31.5 x 41.7cm
Collection: James Fairfax, AO

China
Mallet shaped vase
960–1127 (Song dynasty)
Celadon
26.5cm (h.)
Collection: James Fairfax, AO

Selected Bibliography

Arnesen, Peter Judd. *The Medieval Japanese Daimyo: The Ōuchi Family's Rule of Suō and Nagato.* Yale University Press, New Haven and London, 1979.

Asao Naohiro and Jansen, Marius B. 'Shogun and Tennō'. In Hall, John Whitney, Nagahara Keiji, and Yamamura Kozo (eds). *Japan before Tokugawa: Political Consolidation and Economic Growth, 1500 to 1650.* Princeton University Press, Princeton, 1981, pp.248–70.

Barnhart, Richard M. *Peach Blossom Spring: Gardens and Flowers in Chinese Paintings* [exhibition catalogue]. Metropolitan Museum of Art, New York, 1983.

Bickford, Maggie et al. *Bones of Jade, Soul of Ice: The Flowering Plum in Chinese Art.* Yale University Art Gallery, New Haven, 1985.

Bickford, Maggie. *Ink Plum: The Making of a Chinese Scholar-Painting Genre.* Cambridge University Press, Cambridge, 1996.

Brown, Kendall H. *The Politics of Reclusion: Painting and Power in Momoyama Japan.* University Press, Honolulu, 1997.

Burkus-Chasson, Anne. '"Clouds and Mists That Emanate and Sink Away": Shitao's Waterfall on Mount Lu and practices of observation in the seventeenth century'. *Art History*, vol.19, no.2, June 1996, pp.168–90.

Chaves, Jonathan. *Mei Yao-ch'en and the Development of Early Sung Poetry.* Columbia University Press, New York, 1976.

Cooper, Arthur (ed. and trans.). *Li Po and Tu Fu.* Penguin, Harmondsworth, 1973.

Cunningham, Louisa. *The Spirit of Place: Japanese Paintings and Prints of the Sixteenth through Nineteenth Centuries* [exhibition catalogue]. Yale University Art Gallery, New Haven, 1984.

Cunningham, Michael et al. *The Triumph of Japanese Style: Sixteenth-Century Art in Japan* [exhibition catalogue]. Cleveland Museum of Art, Cleveland, 1991.

Davis, A. R. (ed.), Kotewall, Robert, and Smith, Norman L. (trans.). *The Penguin Book of Chinese Verse.* Penguin Books, Harmondsworth, 1962.

Elison, George. 'Introduction: Japan in the sixteenth century'. In Elison, George and Smith, Bardwell L. (eds). *Warlords, Artists, and Commoners: Japan in the Sixteenth Century* [exhibition catalogue]. University Press of Hawaii, Honolulu, 1981, pp.1–6.

Ford, Barbara Brennan and Impey, Oliver R. *Japanese Art from the Gerry Collection in the Metropolitan Museum of Art* [exhibition catalogue]. Metropolitan Museum of Art, New York, 1989.

Hall, John Whitney. 'Hideyoshi's domestic policies'. In Hall, John Whitney, Nagahara Keiji, and Yamamura Kozo (eds). *Japan before Tokugawa: Political Consolidation and Economic Growth, 1500 to 1650.* Princeton University Press, Princeton, 1981, pp.101–24.

Hall, John Whitney. 'Japan's sixteenth-century revolution'. In Elison, George and Smith, Bardwell L. (eds). *Warlords, Artists, and Commoners: Japan in the Sixteenth Century* [exhibition catalogue]. University Press of Hawaii, Honolulu, 1981, pp.7–21.

Hickman, Money L. et al. *Japan's Golden Age: Momoyama* [exhibition catalogue]. Yale University Press, New Haven, 1996.

Jacobsen, Robert D. *The Art of Japanese Screen Painting: Selections from The Minneapolis Institute of Arts* [exhibition catalogue]. Minneapolis Institute of Arts, Minneapolis, 1984.

The Japan of the Shoguns [exhibition catalogue], Montreal Museum of Fine Arts, Montreal, 1989.

Kakudo Yoshiko. *The Art of Japan: Masterworks in the Asian Art Museum of San Francisco.* Asian Art Museum and Chronicle Books, San Francisco, 1991.

Knoepfle, John and Wang Shouyi (trans.). *Tang Dynasty Poems.* Spoon River Poetry Press, Peoria, 1985.

Li Chi. 'The changing concept of the recluse in Chinese literature'. *Harvard Journal of Asiatic Studies*, vol. 24, 1962, pp.234–47.

Liscomb, Kathlyn Maurean. 'Li Bai, a hero among poets, in the visual, dramatic, and literary arts of China'. *The Art Bulletin*, vol.81, no.3, Sept. 1999, pp.354–89.

Liu Wu-chi and Lo, Irving Yucheng (eds). *Sunflower Splendor: Three Thousand Years of Chinese Poetry.* Indiana University Press, Bloomington, 1975.

Lo, Winston W. *An Introduction to the Civil Service of Sung China.* University of Hawaii Press, Honolulu, 1987.

Marra, Michele. *The Aesthetics of Discontent: Politics and Reclusion in Medieval Japanese Literature.* University of Hawaii Press, Honolulu, 1991.

Matsuoka Hisato and Arnesen, Peter J. 'The Sengoku Daimyo of Western Japan: The case of the Ōuchi'. In Hall, John Whitney, Nagahara Keiji, and Yamamura Kozo (eds). *Japan before Tokugawa: Political Consolidation and Economic Growth, 1500 to 1650.* Princeton University Press, Princeton, 1981, pp.64–100.

Mezaki Tokue. 'Aesthete-recluses during the transition from ancient to medieval Japan'. Miner, Earl (ed.). In *Principles of Classical Japanese Literature.* Princeton University Press, Princeton, 1985, pp.151–80.

Mitchelhill, Jennifer. *Castles of the Samurai: Power and Beauty.* Kodansha International, Tokyo, 2003.

Momoyama: Japanese Art in the Age of Grandeur [exhibition catalogue], Metropolitan Museum of Art, New York, 1975.

Mote, Frederick W. 'Confucian Eremitism in the Yüan period'. In Wright, Arthur F. (ed.). *The Confucian Persuasion.* Stanford University Press, Stanford, 1960, pp.202–40.

Murck, Alfreda. *Poetry and Painting in Song China: The Subtle Art of Dissent.* Harvard University Asia Center, Cambridge and London, 2000.

Nagahara Keiji and Yamamura Kozo. 'The Sengoku Daimyo and the Kandaka system'. In Hall, John Whitney, Nagahara Keiji, and Yamamura Kozo (eds). *Japan before Tokugawa: Political Consolidation and Economic Growth, 1500 to 1650.* Princeton University Press, Princeton, 1981, pp.27–64.

Obata Shigeyoshi. *The Works of Li Po the Chinese Poet.* Paragon Book Reprint Corp., New York, 1965; first published in 1928.

Palter, Robert *The Duchess of Malfi's Apricots, and Other Literary Fruits.* University of South Carolina Press, Columbia, 2002.

Rousmaniere, Nicole Coolidge (ed.). *Arts of Kazari: Japan on Display* [exhibition catalogue]. British Museum Press, London, 2002.

Schlepp, Wayne. 'Lin Pu'. In Franke, Herbert (ed.). *Sung Biographies.* Münchener Ostasiatische Studien. Steiner, Wiesbaden, 1976, pp.613–15.

Seaton, Jerome P. (ed. and trans.). *The Wine of Endless Life: Taoist Drinking Songs from the Yuan Dynasty.* White Pine Press, Buffalo, 1985.

Seth, Vikram. *Three Chinese Poets: Translations of Poems by Wang Wei, Li Bai, and Du Fu.* Harper Perennial, New York, 1992.

Shimizu Yoshiaki and Wheelwright, Carolyn (eds). *Japanese Ink Paintings from American Collections: The Muromachi Period an Exhibition in Honor of Shōjirō Shimada* [exhibition catalogue]. Princeton University Press, Princeton, 1976.

Shimizu Yoshiaki (ed). *Japan: The Shaping of Daimyo Culture 1185–1868* [exhibition catalogue]. National Gallery of Art, Washington, 1988.

The Shogun Age Exhibition from the Tokugawa Art Museum, Japan [exhibition catalogue]. Tokugawa Art Museum, Nagoya-shi, 1983.

Singer, Robert T. et al. *Edo: Art in Japan 1615–1868* [exhibition catalogue]. National Gallery of Art, Washington, 1998.

Smith, Bardwell L. 'Japanese society and culture in the Momoyama era: A bibliographic essay'. In Elison, George and Smith, Bardwell L. (eds). *Warlords, Artists, and Commoners: Japan in the Sixteenth Century* [exhibition catalogue]. University Press of Hawaii, Honolulu, 1981, pp.245–79.

Song Houmei. 'Images of the crane in Chinese painting'. *Oriental Art*, Autumn 1998, pp.11–23.

Tanaka Ichimatsu. *Japanese Ink Painting: Shubun to Sesshu*. Trans. Bruce Darling. Weatherhill/ Heibonsha, New York and Tokyo, 1974 (Heibonsha Survey of Japanese Art vol.12).

A Thousand Cranes: Treasures of Japanese Art [exhibition catalogue]. Seattle Art Museum and Chronicle Books, San Francisco, 1987.

Tucker, John Allen. 'Art, the ethical self, and political eremitism: Fujiwara Seika's essay on landscape painting'. *Journal of Chinese Philosophy*, vol.31, no.1, March 2004, pp.47–63.

Unkokuha no Keifu (Unkoku School: The Successors of the Sesshō Style) [exhibition catalogue]. Yamaguchi Prefectural Museum, Yamaguchi, 1986.

Unkoku Togan to Momoyama Jidai (Unkoku Tōgan and the Momoyama Period) [exhibition catalogue]. Yamaguchi Prefectural Museum, Yamaguchi, 1984.

Ury, Marian. 'Recluses and eccentric monks: Tales from the *Hosshinshu* by Kamo no Chōmei'. *Monumenta Nipponica*, vol.27, 1972, pp.149–73.

Watson, Burton (trans. and ed.). *The Columbia Book of Chinese Poetry from Early Times to the Thirteenth Century*. Columbia University Press, New York, 1984.

Watson, William (ed.). *The Great Japan Exhibition: Art of the Edo Period 1600–1868* [exhibition catalogue]. Royal Academy of Arts, London, and Weidenfeld and Nicolson, London, 1981.

Wheelwright, Carolyn (ed.). *Word in Flower: The Visualization of Classical Literature in Seventeenth-Century Japan*, Yale University Art Gallery, New Haven, 1989.

Wheelwright, Carolyn. 'A visualization of Eitoku's lost paintings at Azuchi Castle'. In Elison, George and Smith, Bardwell L. (eds). *Warlords, Artists, and Commoners: Japan in the Sixteenth Century* [exhibition catalogue]. University Press of Hawaii, Honolulu, 1981, pp.87–111.

Wilson, J. Keith. 'The fine art of drinking: The Chinese silversmith Zhu Bishan and his sculptural cups'. *Bulletin of Cleveland Museum of Art*, vol.81, no.10, December 1994, pp.380–401.

Wu Hung. *The Double Screen: Medium and Representation in Chinese Painting*. Reaktion Books, London, 1996.

Young, David (ed. and trans.). *Wang Wei, Li Po, Tu Fu, Li Ho, Li Shang-yin: Five T'ang Poets*. Oberlin College Press, Oberlin, 1990 (Field Translation Series no.15).

ACKNOWLEDGMENTS

The Queensland Art Gallery gratefully acknowledges James Fairfax, AO, for his generosity in gifting the Unkoku Tōeki screens to the Gallery, and for making works from his own private collection available for the 'Sparse Shadows, Flying Pearls: A Japanese Screen Revealed' exhibition.

Thanks are also extended to the Art Gallery of New South Wales and the National Gallery of Victoria for lending works from their collections and to Dr Mae Anna Pang, Senior Curator, Asian Art, National Gallery of Victoria, and Dr Liu Yang, Curator, Chinese Art, Art Gallery of New South Wales, for their kind support and assistance in the development of this project.

Staff at various institutions assisted with the publication and exhibition by supplying photographic material and copyright permissions, including Alice Livingstone, Art Gallery of New South Wales, Sydney; Debra Baida, Asian Art Museum, San Francisco; Mavis Pilbeam, British Museum, London; Eisei Bunko Foundation, Tokyo; Jennie Moloney, National Gallery of Victoria, Melbourne; and Genevieve Cottraux, University of California, Berkeley Art Museum, Berkeley.

Thank you also to the Queensland Art Gallery staff who contributed to the development of the 'Sparse Shadows, Flying Pearls: A Japanese Screen Revealed' exhibition and the accompanying publication.